When Lions Hunt

Written by Kerrie Shanahan

Flying Start
to Literacy®

Contents

At the water hole

It is hot and dry
on the grasslands.
The zebras are drinking
water at the water hole,
but they do not feel safe.

Something is wrong.
They look around.
They cannot see
anything.

The zebras cannot see the lions that are hunting. The lions are the same colour as the long, dry grass. This is why the zebras cannot see them.

But the lions can see the zebras. They have very good eyesight and can see the zebras from a long way off.

The lions try to get close to the
zebras. They move very quietly.
If the zebras hear them,
they will run away.
Zebras can run very fast.

The lions creep closer and closer.
They are stalking the zebras.

8

The lions are close to the zebras.
They need to catch a zebra. They have
not eaten for three days and they are
hungry. They need food.

The zebras do not know that the lions are nearby.

The attack

A baby zebra walks away from its mother. The lions use their strong legs to spring up and run after the zebra. They will try to jump on the zebra and catch it with their sharp claws and teeth.

The baby zebra starts to run.

The mother zebra sees the lions.

She runs to help the baby zebra.

She kicks the lions.

Now all the zebras can see the lions.
They know the lions are hunting today.
The zebras run from the water hole.

The zebras are safe for now . . .
until the next time the lions hunt.

Back to the pride

The zebras have gone.
The lions will not catch
a zebra now.

The lions walk back to the other lions they live with in their pride. The lions don't have any food this time, but they will hunt again later.

The lions are tired. They used a lot of energy when they were hunting today. They need to rest before they hunt again.

While the lions are resting,
the lion cubs play nearby.
They chase each other.
Then they jump on each other
and roll around.

They are learning how to hunt.
One day, it will be their turn to
hunt for food for the pride.

On the hunt again

The sun is now low in the sky and it is time for the lions to hunt again.

They set out in search of animals. Maybe this time they will bring back some food for the pride to eat.

Glossary

grasslands A large area of land that is covered with grass and small plants, but not trees.

pride A group of lions is called a pride.

stalking Stalking is following another animal without being seen or heard.

water hole A small pond of water where animals can drink.